MY LEGACY EXPERIENCE

How My Mother's Life Prepared
Me For Her Death

By
Donna C. Watson, JD

Purpose Publishing
1503 Main Street #168 Grandview, Missouri 64030
www.PurposePublishing.com

My Legacy Experience
Copyright © 2019 by Donna C. Watson

ISBN: 978-1-0820626-6-7

Bulk Ordering Information: Quantity sales. Special discounts are available on quantity purchases by churches, ministry associations, and others. For details, contact the author at donna@mylegacyexperience.com

Acknowledgements

I would like to express my sincere thanks to my family, friends, and professional service providers for all your support, encouragement and assistance with this project. I would specifically like to thank:

- Ryan Scott, Owner of Market*TING, for my website development.
- Dawnielle B. Robinson, my editor and creative muse.
- Cheriss May, Photographer Extraordinaire.
- Lee Kathryn Counts – Pollard, my technical advisor.
- Michelle Gines and LaToya Humes, for their ministry and service that made this entire project possible.
- Michaela White, my cousin/sister, confidante, and support through every step of my grief process.

My Legacy Experience documents my personal experience with administering my mother's estate. In 2017, my mother was diagnosed with cancer and died shortly after. During her illness, I learned the following life lessons that led me to write this book:

1. *Be prepared to make short term and long-term decisions.*
2. *Everyone has an estate.*
3. *Everyone needs an estate plan.*
4. *Everyone can build an estate.*
5. *Leave a Trail of Breadcrumbs for those left behind.*
6. *It costs money to die!! Who knew???*
7. *Leave a mark and not a scar!*

My goal for this book is to honor my mother's memory by sharing our story of love, wisdom and legacy. *My Legacy Experience* is part personal journal, part instruction manual. Regardless, it is my sincere hope that you will gain something from the read. If you make even one wise financial decision regarding the accumulation and disposition of your estate because of our story, then my mission is accomplished.

TABLE OF CONTENTS

FOREWORD

I'm an only child who grew up in a house with my mother, grand-mother and aunt. These women were my nucleus and we were closer than close. In fact, my grandmother, Cleopatra Watson, (aka "Cleo") was charged early on with being the caretaker of her sister (my Aunt Marjorie), who had polio and suffered a stroke when she was a child. Her life expectancy was projected to extend into her early teens at best. She could not talk or walk, but with determination, love, and the influence of seven other siblings, she learned to walk, talk, cook, and care for herself with supervision. When my grandmother passed in 2006, my mother became responsible for Aunt Marjorie.

Fast forward to Christmas 2016, which was spent in the ER with Aunt Marjorie. Many hours and tests later, she was diagnosed with a grapefruit-sized mass in her lungs. Her doctors were actually surprised she was still alive. Aunt Marjorie stayed in the hospital until we moved her to a rehabilitation facility, where my mother no longer had the option of caring for her. We were uncertain about what affordable options were available and had limited time to get her into a Medicaid approved facility. Needless to say, my mother and I dealt with Medicaid applications, insurance claims and procedures for the first months of 2017, while visiting Aunt Marjorie as much as possible.

Amid the stress and strain of Aunt Marjorie's illness, my mother was diagnosed with a medical condition of her own. In March of

2017, my mother confided in me that she needed surgery to remove a mass from her colon. My first reaction was to print healing scriptures for my mother to read. I asked her to find one that she would use as an anchor for her faith. I tried to remain optimistic about her procedure—accompanying her to preoperative appointments while researching both her surgeon and the type of surgery he would perform. I asked questions and kept a notebook to record our notes in a central place. Despite my efforts, I began to notice a shift in my mother's energy level. She moved slower, seemed distracted and was often preoccupied. In retrospect, I wonder if she sensed her life was coming to an end?

The day before my mother's surgery, I spent the night at her home. She prepared for surgery while my cousin and I prayed with her and kept her company. She was in good spirits when I drove her to the hospital early the next morning. The procedure was scheduled for three hours, but took five and a half. By the time we spoke to the doctor, the scope of the surgery had expanded and resulted in a life-changing existence for my mother.

Despite the lifestyle adjustments my mother would have to make, my family and I remained positive and encouraged. When my mother returned home to recover, I thought I had enough faith to pray my mother through cancer and beat it. Then ten days after my mother's surgery, Aunt Marjorie died. And five days later, on the morning of Aunt Marjorie's funeral, I lost my mother.

I was devasted. I was not sure how to move forward. My aunt was like a grandmother to me and my mother was my rock. What would I do now? How could I move forward when the grief I felt seemed to suffocate me? I could not imagine navigating the rest of this life's journey without them. I knew I had to make a plan and that would require drawing on the lessons my mother's life provided.

While everyone else was gearing up to celebrate Mother's Day, I began planning my mother's funeral. The timing was ironic at best. My mother and I started traveling Mother's Day weekend after I graduated from law school, so the holiday had become quite special for us. We chose to spend quality time with one another that differed from our daily routine and surroundings. We coined our travels to Louisiana, Florida, California and Arizona "The Thelma and Louise Adventures." But 2017 would be different. Our trip to tour the National Museum of African American History and Culture was postponed and ultimately occurred without her.

Luckily my mother had a burial plan, so the financial resources were available. She'd also purchased a cemetery plot, so that decision was taken care of, too. I decided to have her funeral on Friday rather than Saturday because weekday funerals are generally more economical than weekend funerals. Everyone complied with my request that the service be no more than an hour. My cousin was the pastor of her home church, so his support was invaluable during this time. There were many decisions to be made, so I made the decisions I felt strongly about (casket selection, flowers, burial clothing, etc.) and delegated the rest. There was no reason to control every detail of the disposition ceremony.

To this day I do not recall all the details of my mother's funeral... I have no idea who attended and who didn't, what was served at the repast, what was said at the funeral (and I gave the family tribute!) The day was a blur. It is interesting how the mind works in these situations. I was present, but not present because I was experiencing the funeral through a grief filter. I was also in execution mode. I had just enough energy and motivation to take care of a few things. I could not be consumed with every detail of the funeral because I needed my energy to make the next set of important decisions.

A Story in Photos

My mother left a lasting legacy, not only financially, but also spiritually and mentally!

My mother was a beautiful woman, yet very modest.

My mother was a beautiful woman, yet she was never conceited or focused on her physical appearance. I never realized how much I looked like her until she died. This is significant because I feel like her spirit and essence is still with me and I am reminded of her strength every time I look in the mirror.

My mother was present in my life.

My mother was present at every milestone in my life – graduations, promotions, bar admissions, and my first marriage. My mother was also engaged in my everyday life.

My mother invested in my education.

My mother worked 3rd shift at Research Medical Center for over 30 years. This shift allowed her to earn a night shift differential and she was available to take me to school each day. She accompanied me to games, school field trips, and served as a chaperone. She paid for my private school education, which was a significant sacrifice for a single parent.

My mother and I enjoyed traveling.

Every year for Mother's Day we traveled to a different city for restoration and relaxation. We always had a nice glass of wine (or two) at dinner. We enjoyed the beach and a pool with a view. She enjoyed getting a suntan – more often a sunburn! We shopped and always purchased something unique to the culture and city. I have great memories of our time together during our travels and during our entire life.

My mother was a caretaker.

My mother was the power of attorney for Aunt Marjorie. She handled all her financial affairs and took care of many of her personal needs. As a caretaker, my mother was stretched thin and she often put my aunt's needs above her own.

My mother showed me that it is important to take care of your family, but it is also very important to take care of yourself. Sometimes my mother did not delegate or ask for help as much as she should have—which taught me to do things differently going forward.

My mother taught me to be a minimalist.

In many ways, my mother was a minimalist who did not spend a lot of money on our everyday needs or lifestyle. We shared a modest home with my grandmother. I had material things – I even had a few "luxury" items if you will, but I did not have an excess amount of anything.

This lifestyle has served me well. It doesn't take a lot to make me happy. I am able to live under my means and feel satisfied without a lot of material things.

Be Prepared to Make Short-Term and Long-Term Decisions

Chapter Terms

Administering the Estate

- ☛ The process of winding up the financial affairs of the deceased. This process includes paying debts and distributing assets and may or may not involve probate proceedings.

Burial Plan

- ☛ A specific life insurance policy that pays for the policy owner's funeral expenses at death. It is generally a prepaid arrangement.

Executor

- ☛ A person appointed under a will to carry out the instructions outlined in will.

Life Insurance

- ☛ A type of insurance policy that pays a certain sum of money at the death of the insured.

Personal Representative

☛ A person appointed by the probate court to carry out the administration of the decedent's estate. This arrangement occurs when there is no will.

Probate

☛ The process of proving a will.

Probate Court

☛ The judicial system that handles wills, estates, conservatorships and guardianships.

The week immediately after a loved one passes can be a blur, but there are numerous decisions to make. Some decisions need to be made immediately while others can be delayed for a period of time. Do not be surprised if your energy level is low because it is likely you've lost your appetite and are not sleeping well. Despite not being at your best, people are still expecting you to take care of business.

Immediate Decisions

The most immediate decision you must make is how to dispose of your loved one's remains. Do you want a funeral or memorial service? Both require selecting a venue, coordinating schedules, and communicating your plans with family and friends.

You will be asked your preferred musical selections and floral arrangements. What casket color and style? Open casket vs. closed casket? You will have to choose burial garments, as well as a cemetery. Who will write the obituary? What should be included in the obituary? Who will deliver the eulogy?

If there are other parties you need to consult with during the decision-making process, then by all means, do so. However, factoring multiple opinions into the decision-making process can be problematic. In fact, most of the stress and strain that arises during funeral planning concerns the opinions, actions, and attitudes of family members. While it may be awkward, it is always best to start having these conversations before your loved one dies.

When considering all of these factors, it is very important to have clarity about the financial resources available, such as life insurance or cash. What additional resources are required, if any? Is the deceased a veteran? A widow or widower? Did the decedent have a burial plan?

Before you plan anything, you have to have a clear idea of your budget. Assess the costs and determine your non-negotiables. Some think that the amount of money spent on the funeral or memorial service is synonymous with how much you loved the dearly departed. However, I want to challenge that school of thought. If it is a priority to have a funeral or memorial service, do so within your budget. DO NOT go into debt disposing your loved one's remains. There will be a myriad of other expenses that will arise within the first 90 days of death.

Long Term Decisions

After the funeral, the real work starts. The next decisions concern administering the estate. Administering the estate involves a series of long-term decisions. You will have to facilitate the distribution of assets and determine legal title of your loved one's assets at death.

If there are legal documents (a will, trust, transfer on death notations), those documents will govern the disposition of property at death. You may have to open an estate proceeding in probate court, depending on the type of assets you own at death. If there are no legal guidelines, you must go to probate court to transfer title, and that process will involve an attorney, personal representative, filing fees, publications, petitions, and various degrees of supervision.

Your loved one made the choice of estate administration for you. If they made a legal plan or made no plan at all, the die is cast. It is important to remember that if you fail to make a plan, your state law will make a plan FOR YOU. If you have real property, the state where the property is located will govern the disposition. If you have personal property, the state law where you reside will govern the disposition at death.

Read more about administering an estate in Chapter Three.

Emotional Decisions

My mother and I had conversations about what assets she had, so I was prepared to make decisions about her financial affairs. First of all, I knew that I would sell her house because it was too large for me. I also knew that I would give her car to my younger cousin because I already had a car and teenagers need reliable transportation. I didn't have to worry about Aunt Marjorie, but we'd already discussed that if she outlived my mother, I would be responsible for her care and her welfare. Having difficult conversations with your loved ones about their expectations and assets are essential to make important decisions easier.

Now what we didn't talk about was giving away the cardigan she wore around the house when she was cold – the cardigan that still smelled like her. She never mentioned giving away the plates we used for Sunday meals for as long as I could remember. And we certainly never discussed packing the contents of her life, and reducing them into boxes and storage bins. For the first few weeks after my mother's death, I could not go into her house alone. It took even longer to go into her room without crying.

Disposing of personal effects can be the most challenging part of estate administration. You are expected to decide which things you want to keep and which things you want to donate. You have to make a plan and stick to the plan. In theory, you may want to keep everything because everything will remind you of your loved one. In reality, you cannot absorb all of your loved one's physical possessions into your existing living space. If you choose to store all of your loved one's physical possessions, you run the risk of deterioration and decay.

Fortunately, I wasn't attached to too many of my mother's belongings. It was easy for me to separate items into keep, donate, and sell categories. What was not easy was making a decision about each and every piece of personal property in her home. My mother lived in her home for over 17 years. There were items in the home that I had when I was a child, as well as things my mother had when she was a child.

I spent *every* weekend that summer reviewing items in my mother's house and coordinating storage and donation efforts. I worked on one room each week and sorted and boxed all the items in that room. I contacted local charities and hauling companies that offered pick up services. It was daunting, but I had a lot of help. I recall one weekend asking my friends and family to take a shift and we were able to pack and unload roughly one-half of her personal items. As difficult as it was to ask for help, it was necessary. There was so much to do and I could not do it alone.

Decisions Regarding Personal Property

Let's be honest--EVERYTHING will remind you of your loved one. However, it is not practical, nor feasible to keep EVERY-THING. Be reasonable and make a list of 25 items that hold the dearest memories for you. Evaluate the 25 items on that list and ask yourself the following:

- Do you have the space and resources to store and keep these items in your home?
- Do you already possess similar or duplicate items?
- Will you actually use these items?

Unless you are facing a real estate sale or expiring lease, I recommend taking your time reviewing the property. Discuss your plans with interested parties (siblings, spouses, parents, etc.). There is rarely a good reason to drain bank accounts, empty homes, move into homes, and retitle assets the week after death.

I now have select items in my home that reflect the best and dearest memories of my mother and aunt. I also have the satisfaction of knowing her other items are being used by people that needed them.

Decisions Regarding Professional Resources

I used professional resources as often as possible. I hired an attorney, haulers, professional cleaners, and a moving company. I hired an electrician, a realtor, a roofing specialist, an HVAC specialist, and other contractors to get the home ready to sell. Delegation is very important during times of grief and finding qualified reputable professionals is key.

I utilized my company's employee assistance plan to obtain counseling during this time. Surprisingly, there are many resources available that address death and dying. I can't tell you how helpful it was to receive the tools I needed to address my feelings of guilt, anger, and grief. I am not ashamed to admit I sought out all the support I could find.

Do not let financial resources influence your decision to seek professional help with administering the estate. You will have to spend money to handle the myriad of legal issues that arise. You should not endeavor to negotiate property, sell real estate, or initiate any probate action without seeking legal counsel. In fact, some states require the use of an attorney to bring a probate action. It is better to obtain professional help at the onset of the estate administration journey rather than travel down the wrong road and make mistakes or miss critical deadlines. You will pay more money in the end if you have to hire someone to correct your mistakes.

Lesson Two

EVERYONE HAS AN ESTATE

Chapter Terms

Appreciated Assets

☞ Assets that increase in value over time.

Depreciable Assets

☞ Assets that decrease in value over time.

Estate

☞ An estate is everything you own at death including personal property and real property.

Probate Assets

☞ Assets that are subject to the jurisdiction (authority) of the probate court.

Non-probate Assets

☞ Assets that are not subject to the authority of the probate court.

Real Property

☞ Land and real estate.

One of the biggest misconceptions in life is that you have to be wealthy in order to have an estate. By definition, an estate is anything you own at death, so anyone can have an estate—regardless of wealth, status, or social standing.

Your Estate has Value

All estates have value, but the values differ based on the composition of your estate.

Depreciable Property

Some of the items we own are not valuable assets, but rather pieces of depreciable property—property that loses value over time. Depreciable property includes clothes, furniture, vehicles, and electronics. In fact, depreciable property may be worthless by your death. Changes in lifestyle and technology may make certain property obsolete.

Imagine owning the first cell phone created and the first television manufactured at the time of your death. Nobody uses those things anymore. While you may have spent a significant amount of money to make those purchases, those pieces of property no longer hold any financial value.

Sentimental Value

While some property in your estate may have minimal financial value, they may nevertheless have sentimental value. Sentimental value is the emotional value you place on property. Examples of property that holds sentimental value would include your loved one's favorite quilt or blanket, the doll you received from your favorite relative, or your relative's favorite chair.

The sentimental value of property is based on a subjective standard, which means the value is measured on a personal basis. Unfortunately, the sentimental value of property rarely translates into an ascertainable market value.

Appreciated Property

The goal is to have appreciated property in your estate. Appreciated property is property that will grow in size and value over time. Appreciated property includes real estate and investments. An estate rich (no pun intended) in appreciated property allows you to transfer wealth to your family at death.

My mother understood that property deteriorates over time. I recall we cleaned out our closets every Memorial Day and Labor Day holiday. We bagged all the clothes I had outgrown and gathered all the garments I no longer used and donated them to a local charity. We usually re-arranged the furniture in our home to usher in new energy to our living space. We always found items to donate that no longer worked in our home. We de-cluttered not only to preserve a sense of feng-shui in our living space, but also to live a simple and streamlined life. As I grew older, I continued to live in small spaces with minimal furnishings.

I also made it a practice to remove older items when I received something new. My mother encouraged me to keep things simple. We lived in a modest home, and we did not have the space to accumulate a lot of stuff. This childhood lesson continued to play out in my lifetime and prevented me from accumulating excess things.

Know the Character of your Assets

In addition to assessing the value of the property in your estate, you should also know the character of the assets in your estate.

Assets are classified as either probate assets or non-probate assets, and the classification determines how they are distributed at death.

Non-Probate Assets

Non-probate assets are distributed at death by operation of law. There is no formal, legal process (i.e. probate) required to execute those distributions or transfer title. Examples of non-probate assets include life insurance policies with beneficiary designations, jointly owned banking accounts, and beneficiary deeds.

Probate Assets

Probate assets are distributed in accordance with the probate laws of your state. Legal title to these assets are transferred through a process called probate.

A fundamental understanding and recognition of the type of assets you hold is imperative for estate planning. Perhaps your goal is to distribute property with as little court supervision as possible. If that is your goal, you may select joint ownership or create a revocable trust with property titled to the trust.

Not everyone will have the same amount of money and resources in their estate, but that does not make an estate less significant. The goal of estate planning is accumulating resources for retirement and leaving something for your loved ones at death.

Lesson Three

Everyone Needs an Estate Plan

Chapter Terms

Beneficiary

☛ Individual or Entity identified to receive benefit from a trust or will.

Decedent

☛ The deceased individual.

Do Not Resuscitate

☛ A legal order that instructs the appropriate parties to refrain from using cardiopulmonary resuscitation.

Fiduciary

☛ Individual or Corporate Entity that owes a duty to a trust beneficiary.

Grantor

☛ A person that makes a grant or conveyance.

Intestate Statute

☛ State statutes that govern the distribution of property for someone that dies without a will or valid will.

Probate Court

☛ The jurisdiction that deals with wills, estates, conservatorships and guardianships.

Probate

☛ The procedure in which a last will and testament is validated.

Letters Testamentary

☛ Document issued by the probate court that gives the executor of a will authority to exercise control of an estate.

Marketable Title

☛ Title to property that is free and clear from defects.

Power of Attorney

☛ Authority to act on behalf of another regarding legal and financial matters during their lifetime.

Surety Bond

☛ A bond required by probate courts to protect the beneficiaries from an executor or personal representative's wrongdoing. Usually required in intestate proceedings.

Testamentary Trust

☛ A trust that arises from a will.

Testator

☞ A person that has made a will or given a legacy.

Transfer on Death

☞ A designation on certain property that allows ownership to transfer to a designated beneficiary at death.

Trustee

☞ A fiduciary that acts on behalf of another.

Wills

☞ Last will and testament is a legal document that directs the distribution of assets at death.

A huge misconception is that only wealthy individuals need to plan and have the resources to plan. This could not be further from the truth. The value of the estate is NOT the key factor when determining if estate planning is necessary. High net worth individuals are not the only people that should engage in estate planning. If you own assets, you have an opportunity to direct distributions at death—and that is what estate planning is all about.

Despite popular opinion, everyone participates in estate planning--whether passively or actively. If you fail to plan, you have in essence made a plan – a plan that is governed by your state's intestate statute. If you do not create a will, a trust, or assign a transfer on death notation to your titled property, your property will be distributed in accordance with the intestate statute of your state. What is interesting to note about intestate distributions is that they are governed by your familial relationship– no other factors are considered.

We all have family members that are financially irresponsible, or physically and emotional incompetent, and under your state's intestate statutes, those considerations are ignored. Dying intestate allows your state to determine who gets your remaining assets after death and that plan may be very different from your intentions.

Estate planning decisions require thoughtful planning and therefore, should occur PRIOR to death. In fact, every time you purchase property or make a new financial investment, you have an opportunity to participate in estate planning. Every change of life event such as a marriage, divorce, birth, or death should be a time to revisit your current estate plan.

Decedent Benefits

Estate planning provides numerous benefits for the decedent. The decedent can assign future ownership and direct distributions that will be legally recognized and enforced. This power and authority may be attractive in scenarios where beneficiaries are minors, incapacitated, or financially irresponsible.

Beneficiary Benefits

Estate planning also provides benefits for the beneficiaries. The most obvious benefit for beneficiaries and your loved ones is that they no longer have the responsibility and, in some cases, the burden of making decisions regarding the distribution of property. The beneficiaries may take possession and title with little to no legal fees based on the estate plan. Estate planning can often accelerate the timeline for distributing property at death by avoiding probate and statutory waiting periods.

What are the most common estate planning vehicles?

Wills

A will is a document that directs the disposition of property at death. In other words, a will declares who gets what. You can also designate a guardian for minor children in the contents of a will.

Generally, a will must be admitted into the probate court within six months to one year after the date of death. Check your state statute to ensure compliance. You cannot admit a will into the probate court after the statutory period ends. If you miss the deadlines, any distributions of property that would fall under the authority of the probate court will be governed by the intestate statute of your state.

An estate planning attorney normally draft wills—but you can also secure assistance through Legal Aid, Legal Pro Bono Clinics, or Prepaid Legal Services. If you choose to draft your own will, you must ensure the will is valid by making sure it complies with the requirements of your state. Generally, the testator creator of the will must have capacity to create a will and must be over the age of consent (18). Wills must be signed by the testator and witnessed. Some states accept holographic wills (wills drafted in your own handwriting) while others do not. In short, make sure the will is executed using the formalities recognized by your state.

As previously stated, the will directs the distribution of property at death. A will can create a testamentary trust at death, but generally provides for outright distributions. This feature has pros and cons. The outright distribution provides an immediate distribution that is accessible and available to beneficiaries whereas a trust can hold assets for a fixed period of time allowing for both mandatory or discretionary distributions over a period of time.

Assets identified during probate are part of a public record. The parties to the case, the assets, and the value are recorded in the estate inventory and are public records.

On average, you can have a will prepared for a fee of $150 - $250. Many estate planning attorneys prepare wills in conjunction with ancillary documents such as a power of attorney or health care power of attorney.

***There are three additional aspects I want to highlight regarding wills – the personal representative or executor, guardian appointment, bond/surety requirements.

Executor or Personal Representative

The executor or the personal representative is the person or corporation named in the will to administer the estate of the decedent. The terms are often used interchangeably. The executor or personal representative named in the will should be someone you trust and someone who has the capacity and competency to handle estate administration.

Guardian Appointment

When you have minor children, you can use your will to appoint a guardian. A guardian is the person that will raise your children on your behalf. The guardian would be responsible for the care and support of your children. The guardian can be a family member or a friend. The guardianship provision allows you to name a guardian for living children and children born at a later time.

Bond/Surety Requirements

A surety bond provides insurance to the beneficiaries for the executor or personal representative's wrongdoings or errors.

The insurer agrees to compensate the beneficiary if the executor makes a deliberate or unintentional error or mistake during estate administration The errors or mistake usually result in some type of financial hardship or diminution of the estate.

Trusts

A trust is a relationship in which a trustee manages and holds property for the benefit of another. A trust has three parties: the grantor, the trustee and the beneficiary.

The grantor is the creator of the trust and can serve as the trustee of his own trust or immediately appoint a trustee to manage the trust assets.

The trustee manages and holds property for the benefit of the beneficiary. A trustee can be an individual or a corporation/institution and acts as a fiduciary of the assets. A fiduciary is someone that acts on behalf of someone. Not everyone can or should be appointed to serve as a trustee. The trustee holds an awesome responsibility to manage assets and distribute assets in compliance with the underlying trust document and the dispositive provisions. The trustee always acts in the best interest of the beneficiary.

The beneficiary is the recipient of the trust assets. He or she does not own the trust assets, but rather is the intended recipient of the assets.

Trusts can be created during the grantor's lifetime. If the grantor maintains the ability to modify or change the trust during his lifetime, the trust is considered a revocable trust. In those cases, the grantor serves as the trustee. Once the grantor gives up the right to change or modify the trust, the trust is then considered an irrevocable trust and cannot be amended or changed unless by an agreement by all beneficiaries and the court.

Placing your assets in a trust during your lifetime preserves the assets at death. The assets will be distributed in the manner outlined in the trust agreement. Trust distributions can be an outright distribution similar to that of a will or there can be distributions over a period of time, based on the dispositive provisions of the trust. In some instances, the Trustee has discretion to distribute principal or the income earned by the trust. In other cases, the Trustee has a mandatory duty to distribute principal or income. If the trust is fully funded with all the assets you own, there is no need to go to probate court. This is an attractive feature. Moreover, assets held in trust are private and are not listed in a public record.

Transfer on Death Assignments

Finally, the decedent can assign ownership through transfer on death designations or through joint ownership with rights of survivorship. Because legal title passes to a designated party at death, these assets are considered non-probate assets. Legal title is transferred through operation of law so the probate court is not involved. The transfer on death designations are a convenient way to transfer bank accounts and car titles.

Moreover, you can transfer real estate in a similar manner using what is known as a beneficiary deed. A beneficiary deed provides title at your death to a designated party. The designated party does not have an immediate ownership interest in the property. The ownership interest arises at the property owner's death.

Transfer on death (TOD) designations are effective measures for avoiding probate, but it is still important to have a will. There are situations where the transfer on death designations fail for instance:

1. The TOD beneficiary may predecease you, and you did not update your designation.
2. The TOD beneficiary may predecease you, and there is no contingent beneficiary or the contingent beneficiary is deceased.
3. The TOD beneficiary may be incapacitated or incarcerated and cannot take title to the property.
4. You may die before the title is updated with the TOD designation.

My mother used transfer on death notations on all of her assets. We made sure to update the designations when I got married and when I got divorced. My mother did not have a will because she was single, and I was her only child; therefore, there weren't other people to consider regarding asset distribution. Dying intestate totally made sense until I discovered my name was not listed as a beneficiary.

The week of my mother's death, she opened a new bank account to cover her medical bills. She opened the account online with the intention of updating it with a beneficiary, but she died five days later. She never had the opportunity to add the transfer on death notation, which resulted in a one-way ticket to probate court.

Additionally, my mother never filed her beneficiary deed. I found the paperwork in her desk drawer when I was cleaning her house. I know my mother was initially concerned about having my name on the title because it would be an additional asset in my name, so the beneficiary deed was the best option. We discussed the beneficiary deed, but I did not check to make sure she filed the deed with the county clerk's office. I felt such guilt, embarrassment, and shame about this.

This oversight required me to open a probate estate for my mother. I hadn't been admitted to the Missouri bar yet, so I had to hire an attorney to handle the case. Missouri requires a licensed attorney to handle probate representations, so I couldn't handle the matter pro se.

We had to submit a petition so I would be granted Letters of Administration. The Letters of Administration appoints an individual to administer a decedent's estate when property passes under intestate rules. The power conferred in the Letters of Administration is similar to the power a personal representative (someone named in a will).

There are various degrees of supervision required based on the size of the estate.

Because my mother died intestate (without a will), I had to obtain a surety bond, which is a statutory requirement in Missouri. The surety bond is underwritten by an insurance company to protect the beneficiaries from any financial misdeeds of the personal representative. I was the personal representative of my mother's estate and the sole beneficiary of my mother's estate; however, I had to get a surety bond to protect myself from myself. The irony of this was not lost on me.

As part of my probate proceeding, I submitted a petition to sell real estate. I cannot tell you how many realtors and real estate investors contacted me and flooded my mailbox with offers to purchase my mother's home. Anybody and everybody could gain access to the case and determine the value of my mother's home.

My mother was the most private person I knew and she would've been mortified if she knew her affairs were part of a public record.

Some people suggested that I occupy the house or sell it without the court's permission. While some people choose these shortcuts, I wanted to give *marketable title* (a title free and clear of liens and encumbrances) to the buyer. As a result, I had to get permission from the probate court to sell the property as the personal representative of the estate. I couldn't execute the closing documents by signing my mother's name because she was deceased. I couldn't sell the property under my name because I did not have title to the property—hence the need to obtain permission from the court to sell the property. If my mother had a will, I could have signed a surety bond waiver as a beneficiary of the estate. This was a very frustrating and expensive lesson.

*Everyone should have a will that designates the personal representative to serve without bond. Moreover, if you have minor children, designate a guardian in the will.

Ancillary Estate Planning Documents

In addition to property distribution, you should also consider other ancillary documents that can assist should health care issues arise or if you become incapacitated.

Power of Attorney

A power of attorney is the authority or power to act for the benefit of another regarding legal and financial matters. The power of attorney is *given* to another person. I stress this because there is a lot of coercion and abuse in this area. The person giving the power of attorney must realize they are giving this power and must not be threatened, pressured, or coerced into doing so.

The power of attorney allows someone to make decisions in key areas including banking relationships, safe deposit boxes, investments, sale or exchanges, debts and expenses, real property, corporate activities, execution of legally binding documents, business interests, and legal representations. That is why it is critical that only a trusted person receive a power of attorney to act on your behalf.

The power can be immediate (*shifting*) or delayed until a certain point in time (*springing*). Both powers have pros and cons. Shifting powers create an immediate power, which avoids delays, but creates a contemporaneous power with you. Springing powers do not arise until there is a certain event (generally incapacitation), which may need to be determined by the courts or determined by a doctor, which could cause delays. Always choose someone you trust to be your power of attorney.

Living Trust or Living Will

A living trust is a document that declares the medical attention, power, and treatment you desire should you become incapacitated. The term "trust" or "will" used in this context can be misleading. Do not confuse this document with a financial trust or last will and testament. This type of trust or will solely focuses on medical attention/care and should be on file with your primary care physician.

Health Care Power of Attorney

A health care power of attorney designates your wishes regarding resuscitation and end of life care. Sometimes this document is referred to as a DNR (Do Not Resuscitate). If you are seeking medical treatment of any kind, you should remit this document to the attending physician and it should be on file with your primary care physician as well.

My mother had both a power of attorney and a DNR that allowed me to assist with matters while she was in the hospital. My mother created these documents before she entered the hospital and they gave me power to act on her behalf during her life. While she was living, we gave copies of these documents to her physicians and bank representatives.

How much does it cost to execute an estate plan?

An estate plan is a professional service and should be viewed as part of the cost of owning assets. Costs vary—depending on the complexity of the plan, the quantity of assets, and the expertise of the attorney.

Wills range between $150-$500 each. These are upfront costs paid while the testator is still alive. There are additional costs that occur during probate that should be considered. First, there are filing fees to submit a will to probate. Second, there are attorney fees associated with probate. If there is no will, the attorney fees are statutory and are calculated based on a percentage of the estate value. If there is a small estate procedure, the attorney may set a standard price. There are publication fees to give creditors notice of death. There are filing fees for ancillary petitions and reports such as a petition to sell real estate, an estate inventory, and final settlements.

The most expensive document of the estate plans mentioned above would be the trust. Trusts can range from $1,250 - $2,500. Attorneys may offer a set price that includes drafting the trust agreement as well as identifying trust property and retitling assets in the trust's name.

Transfer on death designations are generally low-cost efforts. In Jackson County, Missouri, a beneficiary deed is $26 (2018) . A transfer on death designation for a car is $11(2018). Some designations are free, such as designations on deferred compensation accounts or bank accounts--but of course these fees can vary based on where you reside.

Lesson Four

Everyone Can Build an Estate

Chapter Terms

Bonds

☞ A financing technique used by issuers such as the government, municipalities, or corporations. Generally they generate fixed interest returns.

Risk Tolerance

☞ The degree of variability an individual will withstand in investments.

Equities

☞ The value of shares issued by a company.

One of the biggest misconceptions in life is that you have to be wealthy in order to have an estate. By definition, an estate is anything you own at death, so anyone can have an estate regardless of wealth, status, or social standing.

When I was born, my mother decided to invest in retirement vehicles that would grow over time. She invested in the stock market, deferred compensation plans, and life insurance.

My mother started investing a small, but consistent portion of her wages every pay period. Though her wages were modest, she knew that she was investing over her lifetime, so she disciplined herself to live within her budget, which included savings. Consequently, her contributions increased over time and her investments grew in value.

Building an estate takes time and diligence, but anyone can do it with proper planning. My mother worked hard and prioritized her spending between savings, charity, and household expenses. My mother did not spend a lot of money on our everyday needs or lifestyle. We shared a modest home with my grandmother. I had material things – I even had a few "luxury" items if you will, but I did not have an excess amount of anything.

My mother made these sacrifices for two reasons.

1. My mother determined early in life that she wanted to save enough money to comfortably retire.
2. My mother was determined to leave a financial legacy for her loved ones.

Not everyone will have the same amount of money and resources in their estate, but that does not make an estate less significant. The significance of estate planning is accumulating resources for retirement and leaving something for your loved ones at death.

Retirement Savings

Fortunately, Baby Boomers benefited from working at corporations (manufacturing, health-care, educational institutions) that provided pensions. They had confidence that they could live on their retirement income and social security. For Generation X and Millennials, planning for retirement can be challenging. Fewer corporations offer pensions as they did in the past and deferred compensation matches may have lengthy vesting periods (if they match at all). Additionally, there's been volatility in the stock market and the ongoing message is that the social security fund is diminishing.

With these variables in mind, you have to use time to your advantage. A consistent savings over the life of your career can earn more income than delayed savings at higher contribution levels.

How do you build an estate?

It is important to invest in a variety of financial vehicles to build an estate. Here is a summary of the most common investment vehicles:

Life Insurance

Life insurance is an investment vehicle used to replace income of the deceased. Life insurance is a common investment for someone that has young children or a surviving spouse or partner. Life insurance policies are categorized as *whole* or *term* life insurance.

Whole life insurance is a policy that builds cash value that you can use during your life or add to the value paid at death. *Term life insurance* provides a death benefit to beneficiaries if the policy holder dies during a specific period of time or term. Term life insurance premiums are generally lower than whole life insurance premiums. While whole life insurance policies earn interest, there may be more attractive investment options. Whole life premiums remain the same over the policy period, whereas term life insurance premiums adjust after each expired term.

Life insurance premiums fluctuate based on the age and health of the policy holder. This is significant because the older you get and the more health-related issues you may have, the more expensive health insurance becomes. Health related issues that impact life insurance premiums include weight, smoking, high blood pressure, cancer, and congestive heart failure.

Some insurance companies have juvenile policies, and those policies offer discounted premiums based on the health and age of children. Juvenile life insurance policies serve as a financial planning tool-that provides a tax advantage savings with potential lifetime benefits.

Benefits of Life Insurance:

- Life insurance can pay for funeral expenses and burial costs.
- Life insurance can be used to pay for final expenses and administrative expenses such as probate costs.
- Life insurance can provide a lump-sum distribution to beneficiaries to pay off debt or add to their existing investment.

My mother did not have a life insurance policy for herself. Once I became an adult, she was no longer concerned about income replacement for her family. She invested the money she would have otherwise invested in insurance premiums into other investment strategies.

My mother had a burial policy. The burial policy allevi-
ated the burden for me to make decisions on disposing
her remains after death. The only thing I had to select
was the color of the casket, family flower spray, and the
tombstone.

Real Estate

Real estate is a solid investment vehicle because land
is a finite resource and generally appreciates over time.
We cannot create or produce more land. Also, if you
own land, there may be mineral rights or other resources
on the land that could increase its value. However, it
is important to note that real estate values are affected
by the location of the property and neighboring school
districts.

My mother had one home that I acquired after her
death. I sold the home because it was a large home with
too much space for one person. I was fortunate that
her neighborhood still commanded an attractive listing
price, but that is not always the case. With changing
home needs and changing demographics, the land and
home you purchased may not appreciate over time. The
home was titled in her name alone. A transfer on death
notation on her deed or a beneficiary deed would have
allowed me to avoid probate.

Stock

The stock market is a collection of markets and
exchanges where regular activities of buying, selling,
and issuance of publicly held companies take place.

Individuals can participate in the stock market through corporate initiatives such as deferred compensation plans, money-market accounts, or individual retirement arrangements. Accounts can be self-managed, where the individual directs the purchase and sale of stocks, or they can be managed by a professional.

Participation in the stock market is a significant way to accumulate wealth. It is important to be aware of your risk tolerance and have an investment strategy that supports that. A risk tolerance is the degree of variability in investment returns that an individual investor is willing to withstand. Conservative investors should not have a 100% stock portfolio because the volatility could make them very uncomfortable. Conversely, people that invest in the market over an extended period of time may choose to invest in more stocks understanding that market volatility will flatten over time.

My mother participated in the stock market through her company 401-K plan. She discussed her risk tolerance to determine her investment strategy. When she was younger, she had more investments in equities (stock). As she got older, her investment allocation was primarily fixed assets (bonds) rather than stocks.

Savings Accounts

Savings accounts are bank accounts that earn interest over time. Generally savings accounts require a minimum balance and restrict the number of transactions within a specific period of time. From a retirement standpoint, it is important to have cash savings for emergencies. Emergencies will always occur, and you cannot predict their timing. It is best to consistently save over your lifetime, and maintain a certain level of savings.

My mother had a cash savings account that she had over her lifetime. She used her savings account for car repairs, home repairs, and general life emergencies. It is important to have a savings account for emergencies because they DO come up.

My mother had various other bank accounts because she thought it was important to have cash on hand for emergencies. The rule of thumb is you should have six to eight months of your salary available in some type of savings account.

Deferred Compensation Accounts

Deferred compensation accounts are accounts that allow individuals to invest pre-tax dollars into an investment plan. The plans are owned and sometimes managed by the individual's employer. These accounts are attractive because they allow participants to defer income for a period of time.

Participant's investments are based on their individual's *risk tolerance*. The accounts can be invested as growth funds, which are investments in equities. This investment model yields high returns when the market is up but can sustain great losses if there is a market crash or downturn.

The IRS imposes annual contribution limits to deferred compensation accounts with a higher catch-up contribution limit for individuals over age 50. This prevents individuals from investing all their wages in these types of accounts and thereby avoiding paying federal income tax on their wages.

Deferred compensation plans must be qualified plans which means the plan complies with the Employee Retirement Income Security Act (ERISA). Examples of qualified plans include 401(k) and 403(b) plans.

Typically, companies match contributions to deferred compensation plans up to a maximum percentage. For example, an employer may contribute up to 3% of your salary if you contribute to your plan.

My mother taught me to invest in my deferred compensation account. Fortunately, I have worked for employers that offered qualified plans and employer match, so I have always participated in these arrangements. When a company matches your contributions, take advantage of that benefit. If you don't, you are leaving "free" money on the table.

Traditional Individual Retirement Accounts

A traditional individual retirement account is a plan that allows you to save money for retirement. It is similar to a deferred compensation plan in that it provides for tax-free growth and tax deferred basis.

IRA's are great arrangements in that it allows individuals to invest whether they are tied to an employer's plan or not. There are contribution limits for individual retirement plans with a higher catch-up contribution limit for individuals over age 50.

IRA's allow you to invest without paying an immediate tax on the appreciation. Once you make withdraws from the account, you are taxed on the appreciation. After 70 ½, you are required to begin taking withdraws from the account. These withdraws are referred to as required minimum distributions (RMD's) and they are based on a prescribed factor multiplied by the previous year-end's market value.

You can invest in both a deferred compensation account and an individual retirement account, but depending on your income and filing status, the contributions to the individual retirement account may not be tax deductible or phased out.

Roth Individual Retirement Accounts

The Roth IRA is a retirement account that allows you to save money for retirement using after-tax money. This is an attractive feature for some investors because you can withdraw your contributions tax free at any point in time. Moreover, you can withdraw both your contributions AND earnings after age 59 ½ without paying tax if you meet certain conditions.

As with the Traditional IRA, there are contribution limits for Roth IRA's and a higher catch-up contribution limit for individuals over age 50. Roth IRA contributions are also subject to income limitations. Contributions to a Roth IRA are never deductible.

Annuities

An annuity is an investment that pays a periodic payment over a range of time. Individuals purchase annuities to guarantee a certain income stream at retirement.

My mother had a retirement account that she opened when she began working. My mother did not earn a lot of money but she invested consistently and over a long period of time. Saving and investing became a habit for her. Investing over time can generate more wealth than investing higher dollar amounts later in time.

My mother anticipated her post retirement expenses and then created a strategic lifetime strategy to achieve the level of income she needed. My mother postponed retirement until age 65 so she could maximize her social security income. She did not make withdrawals from her retirement investments until she was required to, which was at age 70 ½.

Keep in mind, my mother started building an estate in the 1970's—which looked totally different from the goals, strategies, and asset composition available today. The point of this discussion is to stress the importance of investing to build for retirement and to leave a financial legacy. The social security fund may not be available in 2035, so it is wise to think of alternative sources of income to fund retirement.

Anyone can build in an estate if they seek professional help and make wise choices over their lifetime.

Lesson Five

LEAVE A TRAIL OF BREADCRUMBS FOR THOSE LEFT BEHIND!

It is wonderful to execute plans, but in the spirit of transparency and fairness, please discuss these plans with a trusted family member or friend. It is great if you execute a will during your lifetime, but if you do not tell others you have a will, or if your loved ones are unable to find a copy of your will, executing a will is pointless.

It is important to document your financial relationships and have your information stored in one central location. Your loved ones may not have the emotional energy or strength to play detective. It is critical to make your transition easy on them. It is important to have your financial information including accounts, policies, and when appropriate, contact names and phone numbers in a central location that is easily accessible by your family at your death.

My mother documented everything! She kept a spiral notebook that contained every account number, and the contact names/phone numbers associated with them. She also had "The File Cabinet", which she insisted we go through before she went into the hospital. I often saw the cabinet growing up, but I did not pay attention to it. It was an eyesore, but during every move, it remained a staple piece of furniture in our design.

The File Cabinet had lots of bright colorful folders. That was not surprising to me because my mother injected whimsy in everything she did. The colorful folders made me smile. The bright colors made it more palatable to open each folder. To my surprise (and with great humility), I opened each folder unveiling the details of every financial relationship she had. In some instances, I had contact names and phone numbers. I did not have to hunt and search for anything. Almost everything was in The File Cabinet. I merely picked up each folder and notified them of her death.

You should create some type of system to assemble all your legal paperwork. Whether you use a fireproof box, file cabinet, or three-ring binder, the point is to make all the paperwork handy. You may also consider using a water-proof and fire-proof filing system to maintain the integrity of the documents if there is an accident.

In speaking with other people, I realize everyone won't have a file cabinet or complex organization system. In those cases, a well-drafted letter may be sufficient. I think of it as a letter of intent. This letter lists your wishes and intentions and documents your preferences. The letter can be used to address a host of issues.

The beginning of the letter should include a statement of love. Reading the decedent's written words can be soothing for a grieving heart. This is the final time you will be able to "speak" to your loved ones, so say everything you want them to know.

The content of your letter will differ based on your assets and your relationship with your family members. You may want to discuss your funeral preferences. You may give directions including contact names and numbers of your financial manager.

The letter will be your way of speaking to family members from the grave. The letter may not be legally binding like a will, but it can provide valuable information to your loved ones during a very difficult and confusing time.

In retrospect, I am proud of my mother and very honored that she accumulated resources and made plans to care for me and others. Jeri had an associate's degree and was the poster child of Introverts Anonymous—but she quietly and consistently prepared herself for retirement.

Lesson Six

IT COSTS MONEY TO DIE! WHO KNEW????

The most common misconception I heard while administering my mother's estate is that you can ignore any expenses and obligations of the decedent. This is partially true. If you admit a will to probate, you must publish notice to creditors. If the creditors choose to pursue a claim, they can petition the court for satisfaction.

If the creditors seek satisfaction, notify the creditors and offer to settle the debt if the estate has sufficient assets. Creditors will negotiate. Some creditors will write off immaterial balances, and never pursue a claim against the estate.

It is important to note you are not personally responsible for your loved one's debts (unless you serve as a co-signor or in some other way are a party to the debt.)

Immediately after my mother passed, I continued to make mortgage payments. My mother had ACH (automatic clearing house) payments withdrawn from her account on a monthly basis. I contacted every creditor to give notice of her death and once I forwarded the death certificate, the automatic withdraws stopped. When I was sure I had a pending sales contract, I stopped paying the mortgage. Missouri has a statute that allows individuals to forgo mortgage payments for three months pending a real estate sale, so check your state's statute because they may have a similar provision.

You may or may not need a death certificate to terminate utilities or other services, but you must have a death certificate to disconnect cell phone service. This was the most ridiculous requirement of all the creditors I worked with. Not only did they want a copy of the death certificate, they also required the obituary as another validating source. I offered the obituary when I initially tried to disconnect service, but they asked for the death certificate. When I returned with the death certificate (which took almost three weeks) they wanted the obituary, too. Most people do not keep a copy of their loved one's obituary like its daily reading material. So we viewed the funeral home's online listing of deaths that month, and they were able to obtain a secondary validation. This process was shocking to me because the cell phone company was a minor creditor in the grand scheme of things, but their policies are common among creditors.

In addition to having access to the decedent's information, it is important to have access to liquid assets to pay for the numerous small expenses that arise after death. There are so many expenses that arise when administering an estate. You will need certified death certificates. You will need to fax documents and mail claim forms. You will need to make copies of every piece of correspondence you send for your records. You may need to pay for attorney fees, a surety bond, or some funeral expenses. You will need to file tax returns and mail bills.

If you sell real estate, you will have to pay for an appraisal. You will have to place items in storage or donate items to a local charity. There are hauling fees to consider and there are recycle and landscaping costs.

Something will need to be repaired or replaced before you place the property on the market. That is just the law of odds. You may need to make repairs that are integral to the sale. You may need to hire professional cleaners, painters, carpenters, or plumbers.

In short, have cash available during the estate administration process because expenses do come up and you will have to take care of them. They cannot get the money from the grave.

Lesson Seven

Leave a Mark and Not a Scar

Death is inevitable. We KNOW that it will happen, but we are often caught off guard when it does. My mother did not have the capacity to make plans and participate in meaningful estate planning conversations while she was ill. In fact, estate-planning decisions should not be made during a time of crisis. The time is now. Don't postpone assembling your documents, drafting a will, or updating your titles another day.

"As a man thinks, so he is." What do you believe about yourself and your ability? You don't have to live in debt or in lack. Certainly it is difficult to overcome some financial obstacles. I don't want to negate the fact that we all start at different entry points in life, but it is important to believe that your life can be greater than your beginning.

Do you have a dream of home ownership? Do you dream of traveling the world? Do you dream of obtaining a degree or advanced degree? Leaving a financial estate will allow your loved ones to pursue their dreams and goals.

My mother built an estate so I could go to school. She wanted to build a foundation for me so that I could be an independent person and contribute to society. That was her dream and goal. She wanted to raise a well-adjusted woman that would build an estate for future generations.

Imagine prioritizing your money to prepare for future generations. My mother did not attend a four-year university, but she imagined her daughter would be able to do so. My mother made sure I had internships and the resources to pay for those opportunities.

Evaluate the decisions you make regarding your resources. Will you be able to provide your children with resources to explore their passions and dreams? I never studied abroad when I was in school, but I will make sure my cousin/nephews will if they choose.

What if you started and managed your own business and passed down the business to your children? Modeling entrepreneurship provides an outstanding financial legacy. My grandmother was a cosmetologist AND a surgical nurse technician. She demonstrated the possibility and reality of having multiple streams of income to invest into her family.

My mother worked for a life insurance agency AND worked as an radiology technician so that she could provide for her family. I worked in various roles in corporate America and law AND prepared income taxes as an additional stream of revenue. I learned to sacrifice time so that I could create opportunities for myself. I work AND I speak so that I can share what I know with my community and beyond.

Everyone has an estate and everyone has an opportunity to build a legacy. The decisions and choices you make determines what that estate will look like.

Leave a mark and not a scar.

NOTES

While I was writing this book I was faced with my own health challenge. I was angry and overwhelmed with the timing because I had barely healed from my mother's and Aunt Marjorie's death. If I've learned anything in the last few years, it is that time waits for no one. I was challenged to examine my life and determine if I had my affairs in decent order. I began to review my assets and investments. I had to challenge myself regarding my rate of spending and my rate of investing. I asked myself the hard question: Are you accumulating wealth or are you accumulating stuff? As diligent as I try to be, I still have opportunities for improvement.

I challenged myself to make changes in my investments and my annual budget. I also challenged myself to review every financial holding, all of my titles, and review my legal affairs. It was more than sobering to discover my mother was still listed as a beneficiary on one account. I now make it an annual practice (every Labor Day) to review my financial holdings and legal affairs for modifications and changes.

When I was a young child, I made lists to keep me on task each day. I created detailed lists that outlined what I wanted to accomplish each day. I crudely drew a check box that I could check when the item was completed. The lists provided order so that I could properly plan and allocate my time against each task. To this day, I keep various lists around my home and office, forever striving to quantify and complete my tasks and goals.

I know how painful it is to suddenly lose a beloved family member, so I've created an ultimate checklist for estate planning needs and retirement goals. The checklist summarizes everything I discussed in this book. The pages are perforated for your convenience. Please use them as a guideline to execute your plan and discuss these matters with your loved ones.

Legal Provisions

- ◯ Draft a Will (copy, attorney name and phone number)
    - ◯ Is the will valid in my resident state?
    - ◯ Is the will signed?
    - ◯ Is the will witnessed by disinterested parties?
    - ◯ Did I have capacity to draft a will?
    - ◯ Do I have an original will that is signed by the testator?
- ◯ Draft a Trust (copy, attorney name and phone number)
    - ◯ Are there any amendments?
    - ◯ Have I named a Trustee and a Successor Trustee?
    - ◯ Is my trust currently funded or will it be funded at death?
    - ◯ Are my assets titled in the trust's name?
    - ◯ Will my assets transfer on death to the trust?
- ◯ Make Transfer on Death notations
    - ◯ Bank Accounts
    - ◯ Vehicle Titles
    - ◯ Other Titles

When I Die I Have Made the following Arrangements:

- ○ Burial Plan (name, policy number, company contact name and phone number)
- ○ Life Insurance (policy number, company contact name and phone number)
- ○ Cemetery Plot (policy number, company contact name and phone number)
- ○ Cemetery Marker
- ○ Casket/Urn
- ○ Cremation/Embalm
- ○ Funeral/Memorial Service/No ceremony
- ○ Obtain no less than 10 copies of the death certificate.
- ○ Write an obituary.

Will

- ○ Ensure you have a valid Last Will and Testament
- ○ Identify the governing Jurisdiction
- ○ Drafting Attorney/Contact Name and Number
- ○ Copy
- ○ Note the location of the original will.
- ○ Was the will filed and preserved with the court?

Trust

- ○ Trust Name?
- ○ Print a copy of the trust and previous versions.
- ○ Jurisdiction?
- ○ Trustee?
- ○ Are all my assets currently titled to the Trust?
- ○ Do I have TOD designations for all assets owned outside the trust?

Personal Property

- ◯ List personal property you want to distribute at death. (Current)
- ◯ Replace names and property titles when necessary.

Property Title

- ◯ Home – Make a copy of the deed.
- ◯ Car – Make a copy of the title.
- ◯ Deferred Compensation Plan – Make a copy of the beneficiary form.
- ◯ Individual Retirement Account – Make a copy of the beneficiary form.
- ◯ Other Retirement Accounts – Make a copy of the beneficiary form.

Annual updates:

- ◯ Are there any deaths during the current year?
- ◯ Are there any births during the current year ?
- ◯ Are there any marriages during the current year?
- ◯ Are there any divorces during the current year?
- ◯ Do I need to update titles?
- ◯ Do I need to update TOD/POD?
- ◯ Do I need to replace any accounts?

Bank Account (Checking and Savings)

- ◯ Bank Account Number
- ◯ Bank Account (Bank Institution, Account Number)
- ◯ Contact Name and Number
- ◯ Estimate Balance/Date

Credit Unions

- ○ Credit Union Name
- ○ Credit Union Account Number
- ○ Contact Name and Number
- ○ Estimated Balance

Deferred Compensation Account

- ○ Brokerage Company Name
- ○ Brokerage Account Number
- ○ Contact Name and Number
- ○ Estimated Balance

Individual Retirement Account

- ○ Brokerage Company Name
- ○ Brokerage Account Number
- ○ Contact Name and Number
- ○ Estimated Balance

Roth Individual Retirement Account

- ○ Brokerage Company Name
- ○ Brokerage Account Number
- ○ Contact Name and Number
- ○ Estimated Balance

Annuities

- ○ Insurance Company Name
- ○ Policy Number
- ○ Contact Name and Number
- ○ Estimated Value
- ○ Deferred Compensation

Life Insurance

○ Insurance Company

○ Policy Number

○ Face Value

○ Cash Value

○ Outstanding Loans

○ Contact Name and Phone Number

Title

○ Who is the owner of my property? Which names appear on title?

○ Has anyone died?

○ Have any circumstances arisen that make me need to change my title.

My plan to build an estate:

○ I will contribute _____%/_____ dollars a weekly/bi-weekly/monthly to a savings account.

○ I will contribute _____%/_____ dollars a weekly/bi-weekly/monthly to an investment.

○ I will/will not purchase life insurance as a means for income replacement.

About the Author

 Donna C. Watson is a graduate of Rockhurst University, Kansas City, Missouri, where she earned a Bachelor of Science Degree in Accounting. She earned her Juris Doctor from Loyola University - Chicago School of Law. Donna is a licensed attorney in Illinois, Oklahoma, and Missouri. She is currently a Trust Administrator with Country Club Trust Company, NA in Kansas City, Missouri. In her role as a Trust Administrator, she oversees the day-to-day administration and operation of various trusts, estates, charitable entities, individual retirement accounts, and investment management accounts. Donna founded The Legacy Experience, LLC to begin a dialogue with under served and traditional communities about money management and estate planning. Donna is a member of The Kansas City Estate Planning Society, The Mid America Charitable Gift Planners, and the Kansas City Metropolitan Bar Association. Donna is a member of Alpha Kappa Alpha Sorority, Incorporated and The Links, Incorporated.

Made in the USA
Middletown, DE
26 May 2022

66243702R10044